Chicken Keeping Essentials

All natural remedies, disease prevention,

treatments for illness, and more.

Sara Grenier Harvey

Creator of the *Chicken Chat* YouTube channel,

and author of *Clucks & Chaos*

Book Cover by:

Fatma Khan on Fiverr

Licenses obtained for cover photos and images

Edition no. 1 2024

Table of Contents

Preface

Throughout my ten years of rescuing chickens and other birds, I've experienced just about every chicken ailment that exists. In the beginning, before chicken keeping became as popular as it is today, and advice wasn't as accessible, I did make mistakes. Many years of research through reading university studies, contacting vets, hatcheries, and companies that manufacture poultry vaccines; resulted in much success for me. As mentioned in my first book entitled *Clucks & Chaos,* I went from dealing with a devastating poultry disease to rescuing thousands of animals; and being able to raise baby chicks without issues. I have spent much time assisting others with poultry issues and became recommended to people by a well-known traveling farm vet in Wisconsin. I wrote this book to share my best tips with you, which you often don't find listed in other sources.

Whether you are new to keeping chickens, or consider yourself a pro by now, this book will give you essential tips to keep your flock healthy and happy for many years to come. I am thrilled to share advice with you to make chicken keeping both simple and very enjoyable.

Creating A Chicken Dwelling

Whether you already have chickens, or you haven't gotten any yet, there are some important things to consider to keep your flock happy and safe. When choosing a location on your property, it is beneficial to find a spot with trees nearby. This will not only help to provide shade when it's hot but may also help block some of the wind during storms. Tree branches overhead also can help prevent aerial predators from swooping down and grabbing your chickens. Just be sure the trees are sturdy and there is not a large risk of them coming down and falling on your coop due to tree rot or high winds. When thinking about high winds, I would not recommend placing a coop next to a pond if you plan to have free-ranging silkie chickens or other small bantams. I have a friend from Missouri who sadly had a silkie hen picked up in the wind and she ended up landing in a pond and drowned. I have several very small chicken breeds that are not good at watching out for predators, so I have a large covered fenced-in area attached to my coops full of dry brown sand. While we were choosing a spot for a coop and run, we made sure the area was pitched downward at the end. This prevents the chicken area from flooding during heavy rains, and when the snow melts in the spring. Be sure your yard doesn't slope down towards your chicken coop or you might risk a muddy mess.

If you don't have a coop yet, or you want an upgrade, one option is to purchase a premade chicken coop. Most farm stores carry several options in stock. You'll find that most are about four feet wide by five or six feet long. Although they are easy to purchase and get set up, these pose several potential problems. One issue is that most of these coop designs are not very tall. This makes cleaning them out a challenging chore. It is difficult for the average height person to stand up inside the outdoor portion of the coop, also keep in mind that while cleaning it, you'll have to bend over to clean the inside part as well. These are also designed to only house two to four chickens humanely. Most people who get chickens end up enjoying them so much, that they end up wanting more chickens, and a large flock just won't fit in these coops. Lastly, and I can't stress this enough, they are *not* very durable. Most of these coops are priced low because they are manufactured cheaply. I have bought these in the past though, to use as quarantine pens. I have purchased about three of them over the years. I found that when exposed to a lot of snow and rainy weather, they tend to deteriorate. The hardware cloth is often attached with tiny thin staples that a predator can easily push through. I have lost track of how many times I have read stories of raccoons easily getting into these coops, and even bears just by knocking them right over. Due to the light weight of these coops, they can also be blown over by strong winds. I wouldn't say they are completely useless though; I have one I place *inside* my chicken pens any time I want to slowly introduce young pullets or cockerels. They last a lot longer this way because the coop is not completely outside in my yard exposed to the elements.

Another option is to find a coop that is pre-used. I have indeed seen some pretty nice coops for sale online. If you choose this option though, I would definitely take time to properly sanitize and clean it well. You don't want to be bringing in any parasites or diseases the prior chickens may have had. The best thing you can use for this is a product called F10 veterinary disinfectant. I have found it available on Amazon. Using harsh chemicals like bleach will leave behind too many fumes that can cause respiratory illness for chickens. One thing to be aware of when buying a used coop is whether or not it is insulated. If you have a climate like I live in, where it can be twenty below zero for days or weeks, you will certainly need an insulated coop. Just be sure that you cover the insulation with another layer of wood because chickens have been known to peck at and eat insulation. This is extremely dangerous and can cause death because the insulation can cause blockages in the chicken's system. People often wonder why a chicken would eat this material in the first place. I am not one hundred percent sure, but it might have something to do with the texture of foam insulation for example… its crunchy like bugs which they love to eat, so maybe that's why. Either way, just make certain it is out of reach for them.

There is often a big debate about whether or not to heat and/or insulate your coop. Will your chickens survive without heat or insulated walls?

Probably. Will they be miserable when it is well below zero and the coop is not insulated? *Most likely*. Especially if you are like me and keep poultry as pets and let them live out their lives after egg-laying is over. I have a few hens that are nearly ten years old and have arthritis. Having insulated walls will also help to prevent frostbite. In addition, I also have rescued a few breeds considered to be *not* cold-hardy, so this is why I choose to build insulated coops. That being said, do some research about what chicken breeds are cold and heat-hardy that will be best for your climate. Make sure you look at several different sources though, I have seen some false information out there regarding chicken breeds. I also use radiant heat panels that produce a low-grade heat, that doesn't pose a risk of fire like the old-fashioned heat lamps. Be very aware that those heat bulbs can and do often cause coop fires! It is not worth the risk of losing everything you worked hard on when there is a safer option on the market.

I plug my radiant heat panel into a *Thermo Cube* outlet. This adapter is designed to turn the heat panel on when the temperature in the coop drops below 35, and it automatically shuts off when above 45 degrees. This doesn't mean that my coop is never under thirty-five degrees, because the heat panel only emits a low heat. The monitors in my coop show that it does not drop below freezing in the coop, so the temperature stays just right for my chickens. I love that with the *Thermo Cube* outlet, I never have to do anything with the heat panel all winter long; no repeated plugging it in and unplugging it.

(Here you can see the white radiant heat panel in the back of my coop. This one is a "Sweeter Heater" brand, made in the USA)

Designing and building your own new coop has major benefits. You can make sure it is exactly how you want it, and there would be no cross-contamination risks. If you are using repurposed materials or all brand-new materials, there are important things that should not be overlooked. Plan for it to be even a bit larger than you feel you need. This way, when you want to add more chickens or other kinds of poultry, they are not overcrowded.

When constructing the frame of the coop, try to use treated 2x4's. Thin untreated wood materials will not last as many years, much like the prefabricated coops I mentioned earlier. It is best to attach hardware cloth *between* two of the boards, rather than just attaching your hardware cloth to one side of the wood. This makes it much more difficult for predators to simply push your metal wire out. Never use poultry wire. It is far too thin and the spacing is wide enough for weasels to go right through the holes. If I could give this kind of wire a rating, I would easily give it a zero.

(An example of the wire secured between the wood sections)

Over the years, when I have made house calls to assist people with their chickens, I often find there is no suitable ventilation. Chickens produce quite a bit of ammonia through their droppings. If there is not enough ventilation, the chickens can develop respiratory issues, and then you end up with sick birds. Make sure your coop has two or more windows, which also helps to prevent the coop from getting too hot. You can also use a hole saw and cut round holes in the top part of the coop to let out ammonia and heat. After cutting out the three-inch holes on our coops, we secured hardware cloth over the holes with large staples. This way predators cannot get inside the coop through the holes. Because my coops have these *and* windows, I often just close off the holes with a rag when it is very cold out, and I just leave the windows open about an inch.

Usually, the first part of a coop to deteriorate is the floor. Due to nightly piles of chicken droppings, the floor will hold quite a bit of moisture. We use a simple method that prevents this from happening, and it has worked for a decade for us so far. The floors of my coops are lined with scrap linoleum I found on clearance sale. I cover these with wood chips, and keeping them clean is so easy! It literally only takes me twenty minutes every morning to scoop off the line of chicken poop from the coop floors, and the linoleum protects the wood underneath. Always remember though, that it is best to use an exterior paint on all outside wood used for coops, and NEVER use cedar. Cedar has fumes that are toxic for chickens, and again, this can result in respiratory issues.

Make sure you have enough roosting poles for your chickens to sleep on. You do not want chickens sleeping on the floor of the coop or in nesting boxes. A chicken laying on the floor will be laying in its own waste, and then the bird will end up with a poop-covered back end, or "Poopy tail" as I call it. Roosting poles are most effective if they are made from 2 x 4s with the four-inch side facing up. This way when it is cold, the chicken can lay with their feet flat and the feathers will cover the feet helping to prevent frostbite.

Some of these boards have sharp edges though, which may result in sore spots on the chicken's legs, so I always use a Dremel tool, and round off the edges.

You want to be sure you have enough egg-laying boxes for the number of hens you have, so they do not fight over these spaces. It is recommended to provide one box per three hens. Some of the egg boxes we constructed when building our coops, but in one coop I also repurposed an old bookshelf laid horizontally. The hens like to have privacy and feel secure when laying eggs, so some people provide egg box curtains or fabric attached to the sides of the boxes. Some people choose to put hay or straw in the nesting boxes, which may or may not be ok. Over the years I had a couple of my chickens eat straw and hay, which caused impacted crops. I like to avoid this possibility and just use wood chips in the boxes instead. Keep in mind that if you use hay or straw, you should try to keep it clean and dry. Wet hay and straw can become moldy and harbor bad bacteria.

Due to the number of predators where I live, which includes eagles, hawks, wolves, weasels, and even bears, I cannot free range. I would have no chickens left. Especially because I have many bantams and silkies, and they just aren't good at watching out for danger, and some cannot see danger coming due to feathers on their heads. I chose to construct large enclosed run areas attached to my three coops. Even though this is a safer route to take, we must make sure the chickens don't become bored and pick on each other. Each of my run areas have several roosting bars, ramps, stumps to jump onto, and even mirrors. Yes, my chickens *do* stand in front of the mirrors and groom themselves. I often wonder just what they are thinking. Some people even found their chickens will peck at a xylophone, swing on a swing, and eat treats out of a metal suet hanger.

(The first two coops we built, with an attached chicken run in the back. Note the large rocks placed around the perimeter.)

(Our most recently built coop is larger, but has the same predator-prevention features)

Safeguarding

One of the most common reasons people lose chickens is due to predators. As wonderful of a creature as these birds are, they lack defense mechanisms. I've heard some pretty crazy stories over the years of predators being able to break into a coop when people felt certain they were secure. Believe it or not, this even includes humans! If you have beautiful quality birds that you take to poultry shows, there is probably someone out there who would like to have your prized poultry all to themselves. Someone snuck into a coop and stole one man's full-grown peacock in the southern part of Wisconsin a few years ago. I also worked for a woman who once told me a couple of her hens had disappeared out of her barn one night with no clues left behind. A couple of weeks later, there was an article in the newspaper that stated a man had escaped from prison and had survived by hiding out and eating somebody's backyard hens. Lo and behold the hens had belonged to her! Shortly after I started rescuing farm animals, educating people, and starting my YouTube channel, I even had a couple of people decide they didn't like me and threatened to harm my flocks. So, as strange as it may seem, I do have coop cameras and locks on my coops. I live by the saying "Better to be safe than sorry".

Be aware of what predators you have in your area. Do you have predators from above like hawks and eagles, ground predators like coyotes and raccoons, neighborhood dogs roaming, or maybe all of the above? An animal as small as a weasel or snake can fit through a hole as small as the size of a quarter. So, use caution when you need to leave windows open. All of our coop window openings are covered in hardware cloth, and fastened between two layers of wood. I once had a raccoon bend a tiny bar of the hardware cloth wire, but it was not able to get into the coop. People often say black bears can be drawn to a chicken coop by the smell of the chicken feed, but they usually don't eat the chickens. I don't like to make assumptions when it comes to the topic of predators. There was a man in a town nearby who had a black bear enter his coop through a window, and the bear grabbed all of the chickens one by one and consumed them one night. He set up a camera and observed the same bear return the next day and remove all of his ducks. Some people in a situation like this decide to contact the Department of Natural Resources to let them know what happened. Sometimes, the DNR will reimburse funds to the livestock owner for the animals lost to wild animal attacks. This, however, is just a small compensation, and is often not the actual value of what the animals were worth… and you will need *proof.*

A few years ago, on a chilly fall day, when I went out to check on my small flock of turkeys, I was in complete shock at what I saw in my poultry pen. I looked over to check the feed bowl, and a full-grown skunk was sitting in the bowl eating my turkey food. It paid no mind to my large turkey toms that were just standing there watching it. We figured something had to be physically wrong with it, because the skunk was out eating during the day, and at dusk, it went *inside* my turkey coop to sleep at night! Usually, skunks are nocturnal. I've known people who have had their chickens taken by wild animals that usually were considered nocturnal, so don't ever think that daytime is safer for chickens than nighttime. I had to relocate my animals into my storage shed until the skunk could safely be removed. It wasn't much fun trying to get my turkeys down from the high loft in the shed in the morning. We have since remodeled that coop and run. Wild animals not only have the risk of predation, but they can also be a risk because they could be carrying illnesses or parasites.

So, what else can be done to prevent losing your chickens to predators? If you choose to have an enclosed area for your chickens like I do, make sure your fencing is buried at least two feet into the ground...the deeper you can go, the better. This helps prevent predators like coyotes, wolves, or even neighborhood dogs from digging under your chicken run. Not only am I lucky to have a lot of sand on my property for my animal pens, but there is also an abundance of large rocks and boulders. It wasn't an easy task, but I placed large rocks around the perimeter of my chicken coops and runs. There have only been a couple of times that I observed a couple of the rocks had been moved by raccoons. But after my mom suggested we sprinkle cayenne pepper around the rocks, the raccoons left them alone and didn't return. I also noticed fewer mouse footprints overnight in my run areas after using the cayenne around the perimeter.

As mentioned, I use cameras in my coops. I purchased three baby monitors from Amazon called "Hello Baby", that don't even require Wi-Fi. The cameras have up to 1000-foot range and even work in 20 below zero weather. I only had to replace one monitor over the course of ten years. I also firmly believe that our motion-activated lights on the back of our garage help keep predators away as well. Pointing them toward my coops doesn't seem to bother my chickens at night, but I wouldn't recommend aiming them toward any close neighbors.

Some chicken keepers choose to have fake owls or use small lights that resemble the shining eyes of predators at night to try and keep unwanted animals away. I've heard many times that hanging

CDs in your backyard may deter predatory birds, although I have never tried it myself since I have my chickens all under roofs. There are some funny videos online of people using those tall wavy inflatable man things like you see at car sales lots, in their yards to deter predators. Hey, whatever works, I'm just not confident my crazy silkies wouldn't be terrified of those.

Using items that create noise can also help keep predators away during the day. In my yard, I have several wind chimes and a squeaky windmill. When I have been gone for lengthy times during the day, I have also placed a radio outside. Sometimes though, you need to keep in mind if your predator prevention measures might be irritating to close by neighbors. I am thankful to have twenty acres, and my closest neighbor has chickens of her own. However, that doesn't mean that I haven't struggled with other people letting their dogs roam in my yard. An unknown dog once dug deep holes all the way around my shed, while trying to get to a rabbit.

After hearing about the incident with the black bear nearby, I started reading about what might deter them. Several articles mentioned that bears hate the smell of Pine-Sol cleaner. So, I bought a bottle of concentrated Pine-Sol, diluted it a bit, and put it into a spray bottle. I lightly spray around the coop area, and I haven't seen any signs of any wild animals going near it. The smell of it does not seem to bother my flocks, but I also wouldn't saturate the area. There are also predatory prevention sprays on the market to deter animals like coyotes and wolves. Many of these mimic the scent of other animal's urine. I have not tried these. I am just too nervous that it might draw in other kinds of curious animals. So, I cannot verify if those work or not. I've never needed to try them, because all of the other precautions I have taken have worked so far for the past decade. I have not yet lost a single animal to predation.

When thinking of safeguarding your flock, be mindful of things like toxins. If you use repurposed materials or coops, be diligent about checking them over for mold. Black mold especially can make any animal very sick and it won't take long either. Other toxins for poultry can be poisonous plants, mushrooms, and chemicals in your yard. Similarly, consider things on your property that could make your dog or cat sick. When planting flowers or bushes near your coops, take a moment to look up whether or not they are toxic for chickens first.

Crucial Supplies

With the ever-growing popularity of chicken keeping, there are many poultry supplies available in stores and online. When it comes to food and water container options, you will mostly find ones either made of plastic or metal. I have always chosen plastic ones, as I don't want to deal with potential rust issues down the road. Another reason is because I use a little apple cider vinegar in my chickens' water sometimes, to help keep them healthy (more on this topic later in the book). It is not recommended to put ACV in metal containers. The acid in the vinegar can eventually cause the metal to corrode, which makes it more likely to rust. I have had no issues using plastic food and water containers for my chickens. I keep them clean by scrubbing them with Dawn dish soap or bleach weekly (Be sure to rinse well). The simplest way to keep the water from freezing in winter is to use a metal heated base. To keep the plastic from melting on the heated base, however, I place an old baking sheet or cookie tin between the water container and the heated base as shown here:

For many years I used large rubber livestock bowls for my chicken food. The main concern people have with these is the chickens possibly using them for a toilet…if you know what I mean. I didn't have this issue too often, but what did occur daily, was the chickens kicking the food out of the bowl. This created a lot of food waste and provided nightly meals for mice that got into my chicken-run areas. I have found the plastic feeders that have attached legs to be much more effective and result in far less waste. These are available in many different sizes to accommodate small to very large flocks.

I have also seen people make chicken feeders
out of large metal or plastic garbage cans, with
holes drilled in them and PVC attachments. If you
go this route, you wouldn't need to fill them as
often, but I would recommend getting screw-on

caps for the PVC ends, so you aren't providing food for wildlife at night.

Using lights in your coop is a personal preference. Some choose to use lights in a coop to try and mimic extended daylight hours, which may result in the hens laying more eggs in the winter. Naturally, during the winter, when there are fewer daylight hours, a hen will not lay as many eggs. I personally do not use a light for this purpose. As mentioned, the temperatures get extremely cold where I live. I feel that if my hens are battling the cold, and their bodies need a break from laying eggs, then so be it. Keep in mind that a hen's body is genetically predisposed to lay a certain number of eggs during her lifetime. If you provide a light for more eggs, you will also, in turn, be shortening the length of time you will get eggs from the hen. I will never become a millionaire from selling eggs, so fewer in winter is really no big deal to me. The only kind of lights I use are LED red bulbs that I do not turn on to extend light hours but rather to light up the coop when it is dark outside due to cloudiness. I swear it seems like we barely see the sun where I live during the months of January and February. The reason I use red bulbs is because they deter the chickens from hurting each other if one gets pecked at or injured. The red color of the bulb masks the color of blood. This is because, unfortunately, chickens tend to peck at others when they see any sight of blood. It is just another small precaution I chose to take.

If you've looked into the options of poultry feed available, you may have noticed there are three basic kinds, but many different brands. The three main kinds of feed are chick starter/grower, layer feed, and all flock. It is important to give baby chicks the proper food to ensure they grow at the proper rate and will not be weak. You can choose between medicated and non-medicated food for chicks. The medicated contains Amprolium. This is a medication that prevents coccidiosis in the chicks. This is a condition that is caused by coccidia. Coccidia are a protozoa and *not* a worm. They survive in the chicken's body by consuming vitamin B and damaging the chicken's intestines. So, I always tell people to NOT give chicks or adult chickens vitamins while treating for an outbreak of coccidiosis. If you do, you are just feeding the protozoa. Another important fact to note is that you shouldn't give the medicated feed if you have *also* chosen to have your chicks vaccinated for coccidiosis. These two measures in conjunction will make them ineffective. I usually have given the medicated feed to chicks in the past with good results, but it doesn't mean they for sure will not ever get coccidiosis. You still need to be diligent about preventing it in the first place. Also, note that other fowl like turkeys and ducks should not eat medicated chick feed.

When chicks reach eighteen weeks old and/or start laying eggs, they will need layer feed to ensure they have enough calcium to form egg shells. If you have a flock with other kinds of poultry, such as turkeys or guinea fowl, *or* you have several roosters, you should choose the *all-flock* feed. The extra calcium in layer feed is not good for these other birds' organs. Thus, you should provide oyster shell for the chicken hens so they consume enough calcium. Some people offer crushed egg shells instead of oyster shell, but I would use caution with this. I once read a story about someone's hen dying from a sharp eggshell cutting her throat when eating it. If you do provide egg shells for calcium, make sure they are chopped finely or ground down to a powder. Egg shells cutting the throat has never happened to my chickens, but I sure wouldn't want it to either. Another difference with all flock feed is it is higher in protein for the other kinds of fowl. I once thought I could get around having to use this kind of feed. I thought I could just use layer feed anyway for my turkeys, but provide extra protein in other forms like black solder fly larvae. Well, I went out to check on my flocks one afternoon, and one of my turkeys was running around in circles. I knew this was either neurological due to a head injury or from a vitamin deficiency. I quickly changed the feed to all flock and my turkey was completely fine the next day.

Honestly, the layer feed options tend to frustrate me. No matter what the brand, the percentages of calcium and protein are all pretty similar. But many of them have corn and soy listed as the first ingredients. They really aren't the best. I try to find options in which wheat and plant protein are higher on the ingredient list. After I struggled with some serious health issues myself I switched to a mainly non-GMO and organic diet. My health completely changed for the better. So, I can assume that organic non-GMO chicken feed would be the best option for my flocks as well. Unfortunately, it is usually very expensive. I have seen organic chicken feed as costly as fifty-five dollars for just 30 pounds. It's not an easy thing to always be spending that much on my poultry food. What I choose to do is buy some organic feed and some regular layer feed, and I mix them together. I figure fewer chemicals are better than just 100% regular feed. I also mix some oyster shell into the food containers.

Every morning, I give my flocks some treats too. I prepare a mixture of cracked corn, black soldier fly larvae, and a bit of oats into a storage bin. The black solder fly larvae are a better option than dried mealworms, which is what most people use. However, the black soldier fly larvae contain a higher percentage of protein and calcium, so they are truly a healthier option than meal worms. I also give my flock vegetables and a bit of fruit daily. They enjoy it and it helps prevent boredom.

A chicken breeder once told me that her flocks stayed healthier when she made sure they ate greens every day. I'm not sure if it's true or not, but it kind of makes sense. Since I cannot free-range due to predators, I figure I should provide the greens they would normally get if they *were* free-range. Broccoli, arugula, blueberries, and banana are some of my flock's favorites.

The following is a short list of foods chickens should NOT eat.

Chocolate/Candy - Toxic

Onions - Contains a toxin that can destroy red blood cells in poultry

Raw beans – Contains toxins even in small amounts

Chocolate – Toxic for chickens and most animals

Citrus fruits – May reduce egg production

Rhubarb leaves – Toxic

Raw eggs – This *may* contain bad bacteria that could cause illness

Tomatoes – Although some people give these to chickens the high acidity is not good, especially in hot weather

Seeds from apples and other fruits – May contain cyanide and/or get stuck in a chicken's crop

Coming Home to Roost

If you keep chickens, at some point you're probably going to want to get more. Maybe some have passed away, or maybe you just want to add to your flock. Baby chicks are adorable and fun to raise. With chicken keeping gaining popularity, there is no lack of places to find them. Many farm stores, feed mills, and farms in your area probably will have chicks for sale in the spring. If you are looking for a specific breed you may also consider ordering chicks from a hatchery.

Many years ago, I did order some bantam Cochins and Silkies from a hatchery. As I gained knowledge over the years, I now try not to order from hatcheries. The problem is, that most people do not order male chicks because they don't want roosters. The result is that most hatcheries will grind up the male chicks or gas them alive and turn them into dog food. I just personally do not want to contribute to that. Perhaps some people justify this because well...what are they *supposed* to do with the unwanted males? If you don't live in a town that has a law banning roosters, you might consider having one. Roosters can be beneficial to a flock, because they warn the hens of nearby predators, and even break up fights between hens. It is recommended to have one rooster per four to six hens, to prevent over-mating, which can cause feather loss for hens. Even so, your rooster might choose a favorite hen, and if she has feather loss, you can purchase what is called a chicken apron, or chicken saddle to protect the hen's back. If you are concerned about roosters being aggressive, I have a helpful video on my YouTube channel, *Chicken Chat*, explaining how to prevent aggression and how to tame roosters. Fortunately, through my work as a poultry rescuer, I also know more and more people who are choosing to have bachelor flocks. This is a flock comprised of all roosters. In my experience, roosters tend to get along without issues if they are raised together or introduced when young. It doesn't mean that you can't try to have a bachelor flock of all males once they are full grown, it's just a little harder to integrate them. Keep in mind that no matter where you choose to get chicks from, the people who do the chick sexing DO make mistakes. The job position itself requires many months of training, and the chicks are so tiny, that sexing them is often very difficult. So, if you place an order of all female chicks, don't be surprised if one or more turn out to be males. Chick sexing is also very stressful on the baby chicks. I found that if you choose sexed chicks *and* you choose them to be vaccinated, it results in a higher percentage of them not surviving the shipping process; especially with tiny bantam babies. It just seems to be too much stress on their bodies. I'm not saying if you choose these options, that they are all going to pass away, I just mean there is a higher risk of it occurring.

Supporting farms in your area may be more of a guilt-free option. I have done this too. However, I prefer to get chicks that have not been exposed to the outside ground yet. Letting them go outside on the natural ground prior to eight weeks of age, makes them more susceptible to picking up parasites and/or coccidia. Some of my chickens had originally come from farm stores when they were selling baby chicks. I actually would help the stores with any sick or ailing chicks, and I brought a few home over the years and I would fix them up and keep them. Just know that these stores are not hatching these babies in the back somewhere. The chicks have come from a hatchery as well. It is not common for farm stores to have vaccinated chicks in the store. However, some feed mills will do this, and some stores will place special orders for you if you request vaccinations for Marek's disease or coccidiosis, for example.

Raising chicks requires a heat source, good husbandry so they don't get sick, and much time before they can go outside. Sometimes picking up full-grown chickens might be an easier option for you. This is usually what I do. I simply search Craigslist and Facebook groups or ask around for any unwanted chickens in need of a home. Nowadays, this is where most of my flock comes from. However, I learned really quickly that I might be bringing in parasites or coccidia. The easiest way to handle this is to get into a routine. I recommend to quarantine all new birds for a minimum of one week. Two weeks is best. No doubt about it, the BEST thing I have ever purchased for my animals is my microscope. Whenever a new animal arrives on my property, I use the microscope to check for any worms or cocci. I was trained by my friend who worked at a veterinary office on how to do this, and I also have a YouTube video on my channel called *"Chicken Chat"* which describes how to do this. Before I had my microscope, I would automatically just treat each bird for worms and coccidiosis, prior to them going out with the rest of my flock. I would also check each one for lice and mites, which I will describe in a later chapter.

In addition, there are often chickens (and many other birds) for sale at animal swaps. Please use extreme caution when picking up animals from swaps. For the past decade, I have helped people with their sick or injured birds, and I can tell you that some of the sickest I have treated have come from animal swaps. It makes me wonder if some people use the swap event to discard ailing and weak animals that they just don't want to deal with anymore. I'm not certain, it just seems likely to me. So, if you don't know what to look out for health-wise for poultry, and/or the seller doesn't let you check them over, I wouldn't recommend getting your chickens from a swap. Especially if you are getting chickens for the first time.

Whether you are getting baby chicks or full-grown chickens, doing a slow introduction to your flock is very important. No matter the size or age, adding new birds will disrupt the pecking order. It is best to use fencing to make a closed-off area for new birds or use a dog kennel or mini coop like I do. Place the new chickens in this separate area so that all chickens can see one another, but they cannot grab or peck each other causing injury. After two weeks, slowly let them out together and keep a close eye on how things go. My rule of thumb is that pecking each other is normal and expected to re-establish the "pecking order". However, ripping feathers out, grabbing onto one another's faces, or jumping on top of them is NOT ok. If this occurs, you will need to separate again and try at a later time. When introducing new chickens, I have had it go very smoothly and it only takes a couple of weeks, but I've also had it go poorly and it takes up to four weeks. Be patient and be cautious, I know it can be tricky, but fixing up injured chickens is even more difficult.

Deciding what kind of chickens to add to your flock can be a tough decision, as there are hundreds of breeds to choose from. You can also find bantam chickens which are much smaller, or standard size which are larger. I sometimes like to joke that I prefer bantam chickens because I can fit more of them in my coops. Truth is, I have about half bantam and half standard size in my flocks. Several types of bantam chickens are considered ornamental breeds, which means they are a fancier-looking chicken. Silkies, Polish, bantam Cochin, naked neck, and D'Uccle are just a few of the smaller ornamentals. These chickens tend to not only be more adorable, but often more docile and friendly as well. I highly recommend Silkie, Polish, and D'Uccle chickens for people who intend to have small children around them for this reason.

Standard-size ornamental chicken breeds include the Appenzeller Spitzhauben, Salmon Faverolle, and Phoenix breeds. A Phoenix rooster can grow a gorgeous tail several feet in length. Some of the other popular standard-size chicken breeds are Wyandotte, Australorp, Sussex, and Orpington. If a *very* large chicken breed is something you are more interested in, the large fowl Cochin and Brahma get the biggest. This is my buff Brahma "Goldie" next to my smallest hen "Sheldon"...

If someone were to ask me what my favorite chicken breed is I'd have to say Cochin, Brahma, Silkie, and Speckled Sussex are my top few. All of them have been extremely friendly to me and they tend to like being handled. They often follow me around and enjoy some extra attention. I do have to warn you a bit about Cochins though. As much as I adore them, with their round bodies, short stubby legs, and round tail; some of them can be quite rude to other chickens. If you've read my first book, you'll know this is exactly how I ended up with one living in my house. When introducing new chickens to my flock, it often seems the sweet-looking Cochins are the ones who are the nastiest to my new ones. I hate to admit it, but I've even had people tell me that their Cochins have killed some of their other chickens. It seems to me though; that they're often the ones who seek my attention and hugs the most. I just can't help but love them anyway. Also, each chicken tends to have their own unique *personality*, no matter what breed they are.

It is probably clear to you by now that my chickens are all pets. Getting eggs and meat from my flocks are not my priorities. Many people, though, feel differently of course, and they choose what are called *production breeds* for this purpose. Common production breeds are the Rhode Island Red, Golden Comet, ISA Brown, and Black Stars, among a few others. These are the kinds you commonly see for sale as chicks at commercial farm stores. Rhode Island Reds used to be one of my favorites, due to their friendliness and beautiful mahogany plumage. This was in the early years of my chicken keeping, and I noticed I would often lose them to illness around two to three years old. So, like I always do, I started to do some research on this subject. I found out that production breeds were genetically bred by humans to lay a lot of eggs early in their life, and then at the two-to-three-year mark, most people just eat them when they slow down in egg production. I have found that breeds like the Wyandotte, tend to lay eggs longer and have less egg laying issues.

The thing is, that when a hen's oviduct shuts down, and they go through the process of not laying any more eggs, they either just stop laying and they are fine, *or* they develop problems in the oviduct. This can be problems like infection (egg yolk peritonitis), internal egg laying, or losing the ability to form an eggshell, even when given extra calcium. I had found that the production breeds (like my Rhode Island's) would succumb to these issues much more frequently than my non-production breeds. It was a shame because those hens were docile and friendly, but I chose to not have them anymore due to issues they tend to have.

If you ever find a large mass under a hen's vent area, it could be the result of such egg-laying issues. Some people will try to drain the mass, or have a vet do this. Years ago, I had to do research on this and try to drain one of my bantam Dominique hens. The process requires a medium-sized needle to be inserted about an inch diagonally down from the vent, on the right side of the body. There is less risk of hitting an organ on this side. When you slowly try to drain some of the fluid, there is one of three colors you will find that will indicate the cause of the fluid buildup.

Grey/green = Infection

Yellow = Egg yolk material

Clear = Water retention

Infection *might* be treatable. When I drained this particular hen, the fluid was clear. I knew it was dangerous to remove too much fluid because if you do, the chicken can go into shock. So, I took out only about one CC, and the water continued to slowly leak out of the syringe hole overnight. I only needed to do this two times over the course of six months, and after I added milk thistle twice per week to her drinking water, which helps with fluid retention, she went on to live three more years until she succumbed to other old age issues. The worst color you could find during the draining process is yellow. This indicates that egg material is building up in the body, and the hen is unable to pass it. It is also very difficult to try and remove with a syringe, due to the thickness. You can try to give additional calcium via oyster shell, powdered egg shells, or liquid calcium to see if the hen can start to form a shell. Usually, however, this is a very tough condition to successfully treat. Keep in mind that there is a rare, but possible genetic defect in which a hen does not possess the ability to form an eggshell even with additional calcium. Such a condition is caused by a shell gland defect.

Hens can lay many different colors of eggs, including dark brown, white, light brown, pink, and even hues of blue and green. Maran chickens lay the darkest of brown eggs, while the Ameraucana and Olive Egger hens lay blue and green. Oftentimes mixed-breed chickens will lay colored eggs as well. I personally really like mixed-breed chickens due to their uniqueness. Some of the most beautiful chickens I have ever seen were mixed-breed. I show many of these in a video on my YouTube channel, *Chicken Chat*. Genetically speaking, when you have a chick from a rooster with a blue egg gene and a hen with a tan egg gene, the result is potentially a hen that will lay a green egg. This hen would be considered an Easter Egger breed of chicken, which is basically a mixed-breed chicken. Additionally, if you take a blue egg gene chicken bred with a *dark* brown egg layer you will get a *dark* green egg layer. However, this isn't always guaranteed. I have an Easter Egger hen that lays regular white eggs.

(A variety of the egg colors my chickens lay)

Be Prepared!

When people first start with chicken keeping, I don't think they realize just how many things can potentially go wrong. This included myself. Until I started doing research, I was not aware of just how many poultry health issues exist. As I mentioned earlier, things tend to go more smoothly if you have a quarantine area for new and/or ailing chickens. Another thing to help you be ready for problems is to have an emergency kit for your flock. In this kit, I would highly recommend having the following:

- Vet wrap

- PLAIN Neosporin

- Rooster Booster Poultry Cell brand vitamins

- A probiotic

- Baytril antibiotic

- Metronidazole

- Dewormer

- Toltrazuril

- Ivermectin Pour On

- Turmeric

- Activated Charcoal

- Prid brand drawing salve

- Denagard

So, let's dive into the reasons why I recommend having these items on hand. The vet wrap, plain Neosporin, and turmeric are important to have for injuries. The reason you want to use the original kind of Neosporin is because the one with added pain relief can be toxic for chickens. Turmeric is an all-natural pain and swelling reducer. I don't measure that out, I just add a few pinches of it to the chicken's food or add a few pinches to their drinking water. I also give this to one of my parrots a few times per week to ease the pain of his arthritis.

The Rooster Booster Poultry Cell is a broad-spectrum liquid vitamin supplement for poultry. It helps boost their immunity and strength, and I have also used it successfully to treat vitamin deficiencies. Sometimes baby chicks can develop a vitamin deficiency, usually vitamin B or E (although it can be others), which causes them to have issues walking, inability to raise their head, and/or crooked toes. Articles suggest you give not just vitamin B, but also selenium to help the chick absorb the vitamin B. The Rooster Booster contains *both* of these, plus many more vitamins. So why buy multiple items when you can use just this one product? Also, without testing, you couldn't be certain which vitamins your chick(s) are deficient in. I have a routine of adding just 3 drops per quart size drinker for any baby chicks twice per week, to avoid the deficiencies in the first place. I have not once had to deal with such issues. I also use this for adult chickens once or twice weekly to keep them healthy. Just remember, if you suspect your flock might be infected with coccidia, do not use vitamins at that time. Otherwise, you are helping the coccidia protozoa grow and gain strength.

A probiotic can also help keep your flock healthy and aid in preventing crop problems in your chickens. Chickens do not have a stomach; they have what is called a "crop" near their breast. This is where the food goes prior to digestion. Sour crop can occur if bad bacteria or yeast starts to grow in their crop. I have found that probiotics and just a ¼ teaspoon of apple cider vinegar help to keep the crop bacteria balanced. I give these two times per week, year-round, except when the temperature outside is above 75. You want to avoid using it when it is hot outside, due to the acidity of the apple cider vinegar. If you find that your chicken has an enlarged squishy crop, this is a sign of sour crop. Some say giving Monistat or athlete's foot cream orally can cure this issue, but I have not done this. Usually by withholding food for 24 hours and giving the ACV and probiotics, along with massaging the crop in a downward motion, has worked well for me. A chicken's crop should not be not much larger than the size of a golf ball for a bantam chicken, and not larger than a softball size for larger chickens. If it is larger, and it is very firm, the crop may be impacted. This means something like long grass, or some other long or hard object is stuck in the crop and the food cannot move through. If you suspect this has happened, quarantine the chicken and recheck the crop the next morning, if the size of the crop has not reduced overnight; it is sour or impacted. If a chicken's crop is too large for too long, it can get stretched out and not reduce in size, which is called a *pendulous crop*. For this, I have used what is called a *crop bra* in the past. It has a piece of fabric that goes in the front of the chicken to hold up the crop, and aid in digestion, with straps to adjust to fit the chicken. I have had no issues with using these, just be sure the straps are not too tight.

Several years ago, the government instated new regulations regarding the availability of antibiotics and other medicines for farm animals. They said farmers and backyard chicken keepers could no longer purchase these things without a prescription. Since I rescue poultry and other birds this had me very upset and frustrated as I often need to remedy new birds I take in. I suppose the FDA did this because they consider the drugs to be potentially harmful to people who might consume the chickens and/or eggs after using the medications. But what about the folks like me who keep these animals as pets and want to fix the illnesses? Sometimes if you want to find something bad enough, you just have to spend some time looking, researching, and asking around. Occasionally, I have been able to find what I needed by seeing if any of my chicken-keeping friends have what I'm looking for on hand. After digging around on the internet though, I have indeed found a few places left through which you can order medications online. If you ever have questions or need help finding what you need, my email address is located on the copyright page of this book.

Baytril is a very effective broad-spectrum antibiotic that treats both gram-negative and gram-positive bacteria. I have used it for wound infections, respiratory infections, and more. I recommend also having Metronidazole in your emergency kit. This is usually effective for treating Giardia (another protozoa), Clostridium,

Canker (protozoa again), and blackhead disease in turkeys... to name a few.

Every chicken keeper should have a good dewormer ready for use. Most people are not aware, however, that certain deworming products only treat certain types of worms. If your chicken has gapeworm, but you use a dewormer that only kills tapeworms and roundworms, it's not going to solve the problem. If you know what kind of worm your chicken is infected with, research what product kills that kind of worm. There is an easier alternative which I highly recommend though. The only dewormer on the market that treats every kind of worm is called "Valbazen". It is not cheap, but it works wonders. It kills not just the adult worms living in the chickens' body, but also the worm eggs, stopping the problem at the core. It also works more gently on a chicken's body than some of the other products. There is a risk if your chicken has a large number of worms and the other products kill the worms too quickly. This can cause a chicken to go into shock. The Valbazen works over the course of a few days instead. It can easily be ordered online, and I am starting to see it more available in local farm stores. The second best dewormer is called "Safeguard", this treatment works for the most common types of worms. Keep in mind that Safeguard is the same product, no matter what kind of animal is on the label. Sometimes there will be a goat or pig on the label, but it is safe for chickens. Although, you will need to look up the proper dosage online, or do the math per pound, of what the dose should be for your chickens.

When it comes to coccidiosis, Corid seems to be the go-to treatment for eradicating the protozoa. My treatment of choice is Toltrazuril. This works in the same fashion as the Valbazen, working slowly and more gently, and also killing off the protozoa eggs. Toltrazuril has worked every time I have needed to use it. Again though, it isn't as common to see in stores, so you have to spend some time online looking for it. This is one of the medicines though, that the FDA says is not safe to use if you plan to eat your chickens. I discovered this medication when I had a bantam rooster with a heavy coccidia load, and Corid was not working. I took him to a vet and she prescribed the Toltrazuril, knowing I keep my chickens as pets. It truly saved his life. This too can be ordered online.

Now that we have gone over internal parasites, let's shift to the external ones. By this, I'm referring to lice and mites. Lice feed on the chicken dander, while mites bite the chickens and feed off their blood. Frustrating and disgusting I know. If you keep chickens for a lengthy time, chances are you are going to have to deal with this at one time or another, unfortunately. The most effective treatment for this I have found to be is

Ivermectin Pour On. It is sometimes located in a locked case at farm stores, which is a blue liquid. The bottle is usually in a small box. You might be thinking of what a chore it would be to chase all your chickens down, pick up each one, and apply the Ivermectin liquid. It sure would be, but I found a much simpler way. I like to empty the bottle of blue liquid into a clean spray bottle. I then dilute it (because this is actually intended for cattle), with about two inches of water and mix it together. When the chickens are on the roost at dusk, I part their feathers on the base of the neck and under the tail and spray about two to three times onto the skin. These places on the chicken's body are where the lice and mites like to hide out and lay eggs. Make sure you apply it to the skin and not just the feathers though, or it might not be effective. Also, this eliminates you having to run around scooping up your chickens during the day to apply it. I also thoroughly clean and spray the coops as well, because the lice and mites will also be on surfaces. Lice can survive on surfaces much longer than mites can survive once off of a chicken's body. Nonetheless, cleaning the coop and pens is essential so the parasites don't reinfest the chickens. You will need to reapply this again after one week, to kill off any new lice or mites which may have hatched. You may wonder if poultry lice and mites can affect you and your other pets. Since most types of poultry lice survive by consuming chicken dander, they cannot survive long off of a bird's body. Mites, which consume blood from the host, however, can bite both you and your pets.

Activated charcoal is something to have on hand for not just chickens but many other animals too. It helps remove toxins from the body. If you suspect your chickens might have ingested something toxic, such as chemicals or toxic plants, giving the activated charcoal might help save their life. I have given it to our dog when she got into the trash, my parrots when they have tasted something they shouldn't have, and even myself. I only use a pinch for a small animal, or two pinches for a larger one. As a side note, you might observe black-colored stools after an animal has been given some charcoal. I often take the activated charcoal myself, after I eat something not organic to help remove any toxins or chemicals.

I would also have some Prid drawing salve in your kit. This helps to treat bumblefoot, which are sores on the bottom of a chicken's foot. Some people apply this and nothing else and just remove the sore and use the vet wrap to cover the foot. I like to use both the Prid *and* regular Neosporin for bumblefoot. I have treated chickens with this problem many times, and I have found the sores heal much faster when using both products in conjunction. Bumblefoot is often caused by a staph infection, so be sure to wear gloves when working with the chicken's feet, and change the vet wrap a minimum of once per week. There are five stages of bumblefoot. If left untreated, the infection can travel up the leg and into the body in the latter stages. At this point, an antibiotic is usually necessary.

Additionally, chickens can get mites on the feet and legs, called scaley leg mites. One sign of this is if the chicken's foot and leg scales become raised and/or grayish in color. The mites like to burrow under the scales where they reproduce and leave waste, which causes the scales to rise up. This doesn't require a medication to treat, but rather a simple paste of Vaseline (or coconut oil) with plain Neosporin. The idea is to suffocate the mites so they die and fall off. I always used the Neosporin to help heal the scales and soreness faster and reapply twice weekly. Some articles suggest applying gasoline or crude oil to the feet. Well, this would probably work, but it is likely your chicken is picking at his or her sore feet and would ingest these harsh chemicals, which is obviously not a good thing. Keep in mind though, that elderly chickens and chickens with feathers on their feet can sometimes have raised scales on the feet as well.

I included Denagard on my list for an emergency kit because it is very effective for treating respiratory illnesses. Note that this medicine often has a pig on the label. It also comes with a preventative dosage listed on it. I greatly appreciated this, because when I was dealing with Mycoplasma in my flock, it is an illness that can reoccur. It typically would rear its ugly head again in some of my chickens during the spring and fall. I found that if I used the preventative dose for a few days during these seasons, none of my chickens would get sick with Mycoplasma again. In fact, I haven't had to deal with this illness in my flock in several years. Tylan is another medicine that can be effective for treating respiratory issues, but it is one that is difficult to find without a prescription. I personally have not had much success when trying the Tylan though, the Denagard and Baytril have been extremely reliable medications for my chickens for a very long time now.

As previously mentioned, having a quarantine area is helpful for many reasons. Not only to integrate new chicks or chickens but also when you have a sick or injured bird. Any time a chicken becomes weak, lethargic, or injured he or she becomes an easy target to get picked on. A chicken presenting symptoms such as sneezing or coughing should be quarantined right away. Oftentimes illnesses like respiratory ones can spread through a flock quickly. Just be mindful that after treatment, it can be tricky to reintroduce them to the flock. In a way, I kind of think of it as the flock getting mad at the separated chicken for being gone, so they often will peck at the chicken upon return. Every chicken has a spot in the pecking order and a purpose. When they leave, they are no longer doing their job or contributing to the flock. I honestly have no evidence of this, but the theory makes a lot of sense. Especially if you have to remove a head hen that was in charge or a rooster. Check on a sick quarantined bird often, as I have noticed that sometimes when you remove a chicken from their flock, they can become depressed and go downhill even more. It may be helpful for you to quarantine but put them close enough to still see your other chickens.

Maintenance

Chickens have their own unique ways of personal maintenance to help keep themselves healthy. Taking dust baths helps keep lice and mites away, so always make sure they have a sandy dry area to do this in. In addition, they preen their feathers and remove feather casings much like parrots and other birds. They have what is called a preen gland (uropygial gland) on the upper side base of the tail. This gland produces an oil that the chicken spreads throughout the feathers. The oil helps repel water off the feathers and keeps them from drying out. However, this does *not* mean that chickens can swim. People often find humor in pictures of chickens floating in their backyard pools. The fact is, that once their feathers do become saturated with water, the chicken will eventually sink. They absolutely cannot swim, and if they try, they cannot do it for very long. Although rare, the uropygial gland can become clogged or impacted. If you ever find a lump at the top base of the tail, or it seems crusty, this may be the cause. This would be one of those cases where I would suggest a vet because it can be tricky to fix the problem.

Chickens also produce what is called a *cecal poop*. Yes, it is gross, and it smells far worse than a regular poop. It often appears runnier and stickier. They do this about once every seven to ten times they poop. So, what is the purpose of this nastiness? Anatomically speaking, the ceca are located at the end of the small intestines. The purpose of these is to collect material that was not broken down in the small intestines, which consists mostly of fibrous materials and it is expelled in the cecal droppings. Although these droppings aren't very pleasant, it *does* indicate that the chicken's digestive tract is working properly.

As chickens grow, they also occasionally shed some of their intestinal lining. This can be alarming to see, as it can appear like there is blood in their poop. Intestinal lining in poop tends to look string-like, and not a pool of blood. This can be tricky to judge, however, because capillary worms look similar, as they are thin stringy worms that may be expelled in chicken droppings. Keep in mind that younger chickens shed intestinal lining more frequently though, and when in doubt have a vet check a stool sample. The presence of what appears to be blood may or may not be a serious issue. Interestingly enough, the opposite is true. I can't tell you how many times someone said to me "Oh my flock doesn't have worms or cocci, because I never see blood in their poop", and when I check a stool sample for them with my microscope and I *indeed* find the flock has worms and/or coccidia.

If you see your chickens sneezing and yawning, this is usually normal and doesn't necessarily indicate illness. These are often also self-maintenance measures. Chickens sneeze to remove dust from the nostrils just like we do. Yawning is also a normal action, but it might not just be because they are tired. Chickens as well as other birds do this often to adjust their crops. They may need to stretch out their necks and yawn sometimes to move any fibrous material around to help move it down further into the digestive system. Providing grit for chickens also helps with their digestive process. Since I have sand inside my chicken runs, I do not need to purchase grit separately.

Every day I make sure to scoop chicken droppings out of my chicken enclosures and I clean inside the coops each morning. New food and fresh water are also a must daily, but there are some important tasks that I make sure are done occasionally too.

(One of my flocks in the clean sandy pen)

Over time, the sand in my chicken runs seems to diminish. This occurs due to the chickens kicking sand out of the pen, and also some of it being removed when I am cleaning up the waste. I like to wait until fall to replenish the sand. I wait until after the first frost occurs because I believe it helps reduce the risk of possible contaminants within the sand. By this, I'm referring to bringing in lice or illness from wild animals that might have been in contact with the sand before I move it into my pens. Does it mean it is one hundred percent safe, no...but I think the frost helps kill off the bad stuff. About once a month I also rake the sand, to make sure it is level, and I remove any large rocks. Many of you probably don't have the convenience of a sand pit on your property like I have, so you might need to purchase sand. Buying bags of play sand, which is intended for children's sand boxes is not a safe option. This kind of sand often contains silica, which is very dangerous to a chicken's respiratory system. Try to find a silica-free construction sand or find a sand pit in your area.

Some people like to use diatomaceous earth, or DE, in their chicken coops and runs. This is made of microscopic particles, that are very sharp. The theory is that the sharp tiny particles can break down the bugs' exoskeleton, and kill them, and that includes poultry lice and mites. Some also believe it is a cure for eliminating internal parasites in chickens as well. Some people use it religiously, and they swear by it. I, however, am not a fan. There is no solid proof that it works, and well, using it can have serious repercussions. I thought it would be a good idea to give it a try when I was new to chicken keeping. As I was scooping out cups of it and raking it into my chicken's sandy areas, I noticed how the fine particles created a cloud of dust in the air. I was unaware of the dangers of breathing it in and I accidentally got too close, causing some to get into my nostrils. Within 24 hours, my sinuses felt blocked, and had pain in my face very badly. The areas around my nose and eyes were extremely painful. You see, if this fine dust gets into your nasal passages, or even worse, your lungs, you can have big problems. And guess what? Not only was I experiencing these respiratory issues, but so were my chickens! Ok, so the fans of this product say you need to put the DE down when it is damp, so it doesn't create a cloud of dust. Well, that poses a little problem. When it clumps together when damp, these particles are not so effective anymore, because they stick together, therefore, it can't do what the product claims. So, I don't recommend it, and if you use it, do so with extreme caution, not just for yourself but your animals as well. I have used it after my bad experience with it, but only *outside* of my chicken coops and pens to possibly help with cross-contamination…but again… I'm not convinced of its effectiveness.

There have been times of course, when my chicken pens get too wet from snow melting or heavy rain storms, and I have to try and dry the areas up. For this, I use not DE but a little bit of barn lime. It is not as dusty as the diatomaceous earth, and it helps dry the sand quickly. Just be aware that a little bit goes a long way. If you use a lot of it, the ground will get extremely hard. I made that mistake and now I have a few spots where the sand got so hard the chickens can't dust bathe in those spots. There is plenty of room to dust bathe elsewhere, I just make sure now that I only sprinkle a little bit when the sand is really muddy.

As far as dwelling maintenance goes, I also check ramps and roosting poles every once in a while, to make sure there are no sharp areas or splinters. It is easier to take a quick look at these areas than it is to have to treat a bunch of chickens with bumblefoot. Often after I lock all my birds up at night, I also take a moment to look for any areas around the perimeter where predators, or even the chickens, might have dug any holes leaving a security gap. This goes hand in hand with making sure windows and latches are secure and working properly.

Another very important part of maintenance that I do for my chickens, is what I call "Chicken Checks". Take note that this is the very same process I go through when I find an ailing chicken. Think of it as a sick chicken checklist.

Every one to two months I do health checks on either all of my chickens or most of my chickens. I start by checking for lice and mites on the skin at the base of the neck and under the tail. This is where lice and mites like to hide out and lay eggs to produce even more creepy crawlers. As previously mentioned, if I do find any of these bugs, I use the Ivermectin Pour On.

Next, I check the chicken's crop on the front, just under the neck. Does it seem to be an appropriate size? Be sure the crop is not too large and squishy, or very hard due to an impaction or sour crop. As noted, separate the chicken if a crop issue is present.

Weight checks are also important periodically. A thin chicken may have underlying issues and it could indicate that the chicken is not eating properly. To check the weight, you need to feel under the chicken for the keel bone. This is a sharp long bone that runs underneath the midline of the chicken. You should feel muscle mass along each side of this bone. If the muscle protrudes out much farther than the keel bone, the bird could be a bit overweight. If you do not feel much muscle, and the keel bone protrudes out further and feels very sharp, the chicken is underweight. Again, the same is true for judging the weight of parrot species. When in doubt, you can look online for what the weight of your particular breed of chicken should be, and place them on a scale. I had a vet once tell me that when a chicken becomes too thin, and the bone is sticking far out, it becomes very hard to fix any illness. I have found this to be true. I have also had a couple of incidents in which I have an elderly hen that eats well, and I could not indicate any health issues, but they become very thin and lethargic. It seemed like once they started to lose weight, they just continued to become weak and waste away.

After I check these things, I move on to the chicken's feet, checking for bumblefoot. If there are any dark-colored sores on the bottom of the foot, you need to do a bumblefoot treatment. I do not separate the chicken for this, as if the sores are wrapped properly with vet wrap, they are not contagious. I like to check the toenails too. Yes, sometimes chickens need to have their nails trimmed. I use the same clipper as you would use for dogs. And just like with dogs, the toenails have a quick that you do not want to cut into or it will bleed. To avoid this, I just clip the very ends of the nails. If a chicken's nails do get too long, and they are not trimmed, they could entirely break off, especially when jumping off of a roost. This might not seem like a big deal, but I'll warn you when an entire nail breaks off, it bleeds… and it bleeds a lot! They also run the risk of the open area becoming infected. To stop bleeding, you can use cornstarch and apply pressure to the area. I personally would try to wrap the end of the toe to avoid possible infection.

The last thing I check either for my monthly checks or when looking over a sick chicken, is the area under the tail. Does the chicken have poop stuck to its bum? If it does, this will need to be washed, and feathers trimmed. A poopy backside is usually an indicator that the chicken could have coccidiosis, worms, or a fungal or bacterial issue. The reason I trim feathers when this happens is because the issue will take time to fix, and until it is fixed, the poop will continue to stick to this area. Oftentimes it is due to runny droppings. This also can occur, however, if you have the silkie breed of chicken because they have so many fluffy feathers near their vent (place where poop is expelled). If a chicken does not roost and lays down at night, they might also have a soiled bottom. Whatever the cause, trust me, just trim it or it will happen again.

To effectively rule out the parasite and cocci possibility, I use a microscope. It wasn't all that difficult to learn how to check fecal samples with my scope. It has undoubtedly been the best thing I have purchased for my animals. I no longer have to make guesses as to if they have parasites or not. I spent about three hundred on the microscope, but it was well worth the money. If you decide to try using one as well, the only other cost involved is for ordering the supplies you will need. Sterile test tubes, microscope slides, slide covers, and fecal float solution will be necessary. The float solution is a bit expensive, but the bottle will last a very long time. I have read articles that suggest using a homemade salt solution is a cheaper option. However, I would think if you do not make this solution exactly how it needs to be, you may have trouble getting accurate results.

I have a YouTube video that teaches viewers how to properly use a microscope and check chicken stool samples. If you search online for "Chicken parasite eggs under a microscope", you can see what they might look like when you do your testing. Each type of worm egg does look similar to others, but there are a few differences. For example, cecal worm eggs and tapeworm eggs both have an elongated shape... but the tapeworm egg has tiny caps on each end of it. There are useful parasite worm egg charts available on the internet in which you can make comparisons to what you are seeing on the microscope slide. Coccidia eggs are easily identifiable, as they are much smaller than worm eggs and are mostly round. I often check my flock's stool samples routinely in the spring and fall, when these issues are more common. Of course, I also do the test any time I see a lethargic, or sick-looking chicken. A few months ago, my daughter bought a juvenile bearded dragon, and we noticed she was not as active as she should have been. Upon doing the microscope check, I found the lizard to be *full* of BOTH worm eggs and coccidia. Had I not had the option to check a sample, we wouldn't have known how to treat the bearded dragon, and she might not have survived this large load of parasites.

There are several all-natural ways to help prevent your flock from getting internal worms and coccidiosis. I sprinkle just a bit of garlic, cayenne pepper, and oregano on my chicken's food twice per week. Chickens only have around three hundred taste buds, unlike humans which have several thousand. They do not taste spice or garlic like we do. Some say that if you give these spices too often the hens might start to develop soft-shelled eggs, but in my ten years of having chickens, I have never found that to be the case. In fact, since I started giving these spices for parasite prevention, I rarely ever find an outbreak on my property, unless I bring in new chickens, or very young chickens that are already carrying the worms and/or cocci. During ancient Egyptian times, humans would place minced garlic in their shoes for parasite treatment. The theory is that the garlic would enter the bloodstream through the feet. Some say pumpkin works as well to prevent worms. Just keep in mind that these are preventatives and *not* cures. If your chicken(s) have an active heavy load of parasites, they *will* need a medication for treatment.

To keep flies, mosquitoes, and other insects away from my coop, I like to use essential oils. Several oils help repel these kinds of pests.

I simply mix about ten drops of the following oils into a spray bottle diluted with a little water:

Lavender

Lemongrass

Oregano

Cinnamon

Eucalyptus

Tea Tree Oil

It works well and leaves the coop smelling nice. It does not seem to bother the chickens' respiratory systems, but I would not saturate the coop. I just spray a few times inside and outside around the perimeter.

After you have chickens for a while, you might notice the hens sometimes become broody. This is when their motherly instinct kicks in, and they want to sit on eggs and let them hatch. They sometimes become so determined to do so, that they would sit on golf balls or fake eggs. I even once had a silkie hen sitting on a large ball of poop trying to hatch that! This being said, breeds like cochins and silkies tend to go into broody mode way more often than other breeds. If you do not want to let them hatch chicks, it is important to try and break them of this habit for several reasons. One is because a broody hen does not come off the nest as much to eat, drink, and take dust baths, which makes them more prone to catching illness and lice. The other is because some hens can be so determined they will literally sit there for months!

Breaking a hen of broodiness can take time, but doesn't have to be difficult. When a hen is broody, her body temperature will rise to keep the eggs warm. So, one method is to try and reduce her body temperature. I always remove the hen from the coop, and place her in a dog kennel in my garage or basement (but not in the dark), where it is a little cooler. I once read an article that suggested placing a broody hen on ice. Please! Do not do this! If a chicken's body temperature is reduced too quickly, they can go into shock. The same is true if it is extremely hot outside and you give chickens ice water. Many people do that and say it's safe, but again, any *drastic* change in body temperature does not come without risk. Another way that I have successfully broken broodiness, is to provide plenty of distractions. Giving extra vegetables and fruits, and even things the chicken may have never tried eating before. It helps greatly to try and get their mind off of just sitting on eggs. You could also try a plastic treat ball made for chickens. The more distractions the better! These methods usually work for my hens without too much trouble.

As you can tell by now, there are many types of maintenance you should do for your chicken flock and their living space. Perhaps it seems like a lot of work, but I find things go much more smoothly if you stay on top of things and get into a routine. I definitely find it is much easier to prevent problems in the first place, rather than trying to fix problems when they occur.

Disease Prevention & Treatment

Using caution when bringing home new chickens, and keeping their areas clean are two ways to keep your risk of disease low. Most people can avoid poultry diseases by practicing these measures. However, it is important to have a general knowledge of how diseases can spread, and how to prevent and treat them if such problems arise in your flock. The following are some of the more common poultry diseases:

Marek's Disease: Unfortunately, I have dealt with this one in my flock, as mentioned in my first book, "Clucks & Chaos". There are many myths out there regarding this disease. Marek's is a herpes virus that causes tumor-like lesions within the chicken's body, which eventually causes lameness and paralysis. Think of it like the "Cancer" in the world of chickens. Some articles suggest that a classic sign is one of the chicken's legs will stick out to the front, and the other toward the back, kind of like they are doing the splits. However, I did not observe this with my flock. More commonly, it would start with the chicken limping, and not eating as much, and then they would start to waste away. During this process, you might also find green-colored droppings. This is the result of the chicken not eating enough and bile forming in the poop.

Marek's is spread by chicken dander in the air, so once the disease is on your property, it is nearly impossible to get rid of. It can spread via wild birds, or even on your clothes if you have handled birds infected with the disease. Other misinformation out there is that only young chickens can contract and succumb to Marek's disease. I can assure you that I indeed had adult chickens pass away from it in my flock. The good news is that there is a Marek's vaccine option at most hatcheries, and you can also purchase the vaccine online yourself. It is most effective when given to chicks within 24 hours after hatching, and the vaccine solution does start to deactivate within one hour after mixing the contents together. I have had good results vaccinating adult chickens in my flock, and also by giving a yearly booster. Most people like to argue that those methods are ineffective, but I know it worked for me. There is no documented treatment for Marek's. However, I also made sure my flock was getting vitamins, and probiotics biweekly, to keep their immune systems strong. In my first book, I also mention some other unorthodox treatments I used to try and prevent the rest of my flock from dying of Marek's disease. I was able to go from losing half my flock, to zero deaths and being able to raise chicks on my property with no more losses to the disease.

There is also an ocular form of Marek's which primarily affects the eyes. It is easy to tell if your chickens have this because the pupil of the eye will become misshapen. It will no longer be round but can turn into an oval or uneven circle. This form of the disease is usually not fatal, whereas the more common form of Marek's disease has a high mortality rate. Marek's can only be verified by sending in a deceased chicken's body for lab testing. Some veterinary offices will help you do this, or you can try calling a university in your state that has a veterinary poultry extension, and see if you can send in the chicken yourself and work with them directly.

Mycoplasma: In many chicken flocks where Marek's disease is prevalent, the chickens also seem to contract mycoplasma (although flocks without Marek's can get this disease too). This is most likely due to their compromised immune systems, and mycoplasma can be a more common respiratory disease in the environment. Chickens can become infected with this disease from other birds that may not even appear symptomatic. It spreads through the air, direct contact, nasal fluids, and droppings. As if Marek's isn't devastating and challenging enough, I also had to deal with my chickens being sick with mycoplasma. This was also verified by lab testing.

Symptoms observed were nasal and eye discharge, bubbles in the eyes, raspy breathing, swollen face, and coughing sounds. I was able to remedy this quite quickly and effectively by dosing my flock with Denagard. I also purchased a product called "VetRx". This is similar to "Vick's Vapor Rub" for humans. So, the same concept applies, you rub it on the chicken's comb and wattles to aid with breathing. I also would put a few dabs of it on my chicken's perches at night. When I had a chicken that was having a very hard time breathing, I would also try to boost their immune system by putting a little elderberry, and echinacea on a piece of bread and feeding it to them. By using the preventative dose of Denagard every spring and fall, I have not had a chicken sick with mycoplasma in many years. If you don't keep on top of their health, it is a disease that can reoccur, so always keep that in mind. Some hatcheries and online farm websites do have a vaccine for this disease available. Some people have also said they've had success using Tylan as a treatment. I, however, have never found that medicine to be effective for any illness in my ten years of having chickens. Personally, if I couldn't use the Denagard, my next choice would be Baytril.

Infectious Bronchitis: Infectious bronchitis is also spread from chicken to chicken in the same ways as mycoplasma, via feces, respiratory discharges, or through the air. It is also similar in the fact that the symptoms are generally the same.

However, you might also find that the hens start to lay thin-shelled eggs or eggs that have a wrinkled shell. There is a vaccine available for this disease too, but you don't want to overload a chick's delicate system and choose too many vaccines, I would only recommend this vaccine, or the other respiratory vaccines, *if* you have verified one of these diseases have been present in your flock. Denagard or Baytril medicines might be effective for treating this disease, along with the VetRx and other supportive care.

Coryza: With this respiratory disease yet again you may find nasal discharge, raspy breathing, and the other symptoms previously mentioned. You can often distinguish coryza from the other respiratory diseases though, because it frequently causes diarrhea and a foul-smelling discharge seeping from the eyes and/or nasal passages. I never observed a foul smell when my chickens were symptomatic with mycoplasma. A vaccine is available for this as well. Denagard and Baytril are *not* known to treat this disease. However, erythromycin or oxytetracycline might be effective. I would recommend the VetRx and supportive care for this illness as well.

Fowl pox: Fowl pox is not a respiratory disease, but rather a viral infection that causes lesions on the chicken's face, respiratory system, and gastrointestinal tracts. There are two forms of this disease, cutaneous (also known as dry pox), and diphtheric (or wet pox). With the dry pox illness, you will see white blister-like lesions on the chicken's comb, wattles, and/or eye areas. These lesions often turn black and fall off after several weeks. The wet pox will present itself as yellowish lesions in the mouth and/or throat. This can cause difficulty breathing and eating and can be more likely fatal than dry pox. In extreme cases, the lesions were also found in the internal organs upon necropsy (autopsy of deceased chicken). This disease is commonly caused by mosquitos biting the chickens but is also highly contagious from other birds. Meaning, that much like many other illnesses and parasites, wild birds carrying this disease can spread it to your flock. There is a vaccine for this, and honestly, with the high number of mosquitos where I live, I would choose this vaccine if I didn't already have to use the Marek's vaccine due to it being on my property years ago. As mentioned, I wouldn't recommend giving chicks too many vaccinations at once.

There are no effective medicines documented to cure this disease. Every article I have read over the years has suggested to just "let fowl pox run its course". I have to disagree with this. Any time my chickens are sick and suffering I feel like I can't just stand by and do nothing to try and help. The pox lesions can be painful. I personally would put plain Neosporin on the lesions, and try to boost their immune systems, so they are more likely to recover faster. I often give just a bit of elderberry, echinacea, olive leaf, oregano, and probiotics whenever I have sick chickens. Some people have said applying plain toothpaste to the lesions helps dry them up much faster, however, I have not tried this myself, so I cannot verify its effectiveness. I also would not put the toothpaste in the mouth or nasal cavities, because it probably should not be ingested.

Botulism: This is a very dangerous toxin, produced by bacteria. Remember me saying how important it is for disease prevention to keep a clean coop? This is one reason why. Dirty conditions or rotting food can produce the bacteria that cause botulism. Signs of this illness would include partial paralysis, inability to stand, labored breathing, and weakness. The chickens would somewhat seem to be in a drunken-like state. This is due to the neurotoxins affecting the brain. If birds survive for 48 hours, they might be able to recover. There is no vaccine to prevent it, but once affected, some have had success with giving botulism antitoxin injections. Encouraging more fluids to try and flush out the toxins, and activated charcoal might aid in recovery.

Newcastle disease: This is a very contagious and frequently fatal disease. The good news is that it isn't very common in the United States. There were only a few documented sporadic cases in the 1970s, and early 2000s and none since 2020 which was in California. This disease is considered to be reportable. Meaning, that if you have a verified case of it, you are required to report it to the USDA. Symptoms include lethargy, labored breathing with mucous, spasms, paralysis, and sudden death. There is no documented treatment for this disease. There is a vaccine available for Newcastle disease. I have never vaccinated for this, as I do not believe there has ever been a case of it in the state I live in. If I lived in California though, and there were cases of it in my area, I might consider it. Wild birds can carry Newcastle and spread it also.

Avian Influenza: Also known as the *bird flu*, avian influenza is another serious and reportable disease. I did an interview on my YouTube channel with a man from New York who experienced the devastation of dealing with this disease. It is often carried by wild geese, and since his poultry pens were not covered, he believed that is how his birds got the virus. Once you tell the USDA that you have cases of avian influenza on your property, they will show up and euthanize all birds... and there seem to be no exceptions. One of the questions I asked him was if a person had birds inside their house and if the government would euthanize those as well. He told me he believed they would, because they entered his home, and turned off his incubators which had developing chicks inside.

This was a very interesting interview for me because there had been a lot of controversy around the bird flu. Some people believed it was a government conspiracy, and that they were mass killing poultry to disrupt our food supply on purpose. To be quite frank, I am one to not be very trusting of our government, but after speaking with this man and hearing his heartbreaking story, I do not agree it is a conspiracy. The symptoms he described were common symptoms documented for this illness. They include the chickens' comb and wattles turning blue/purple, low energy and appetite, lack of coordination, diarrhea, nasal discharge, and inability to breathe. Symptoms come on rapidly and often cause sudden death. Just overnight, the man I interviewed said many of his chickens had died. After he reported it, the government showed up in hazmat suits, put the rest of his birds in barrels covered with a lid, and inserted a hose to euthanize them by gassing. He told me he did want to start over with chickens in the future, but was required by law to wait a certain amount of time.

There is a vaccine for this disease as well. However, there are simple steps you can take to avoid your flock contracting it. If you live in an area where wild birds, especially geese, fly over during migration times, keep your poultry pens covered. I would not free range during these times, especially if you see geese landing in your yard. If I see wild geese in my yard, I don't even walk in that area, due to possible cross-contamination. Avian influenza most commonly spreads through the droppings of infected birds. I also would not swap poultry with anyone during migration periods. I don't mean to sound paranoid, but I would be devastated to lose my

flock to the bird flu, and my heart would break if
the government showed up and euthanized my
innocent indoor parrots.

Aspergillosis: Also called *brooder pneumonia,*
aspergillosis is caused by a fungal infection. Yet
another reason to keep your coops and brooders
clean and dry! Chickens can become ill with
aspergillosis from fungus in the food or bedding.
Symptoms of this include suppressed growth,
emaciation, increased thirst, weakness, rapid
breathing, and/or tremors. With this illness, it may
not be obvious what the cause is at first. But with
any sickness, it is always important to do a full
cleaning of the area and replace food and water.
There is no vaccine for this disease. After doing a
thorough cleaning and making sure there is
suitable ventilation, I would however try the
activated charcoal to remove toxins from the body.
I would also incorporate a few drops of aloe and

apple cider vinegar into the drinking water, as these are known to kill various types of fungus.

Poultry Worm Information

Following are the most common kinds of poultry worms, what they look like, and how they affect a chicken's body:

Roundworms: If a chicken has a heavy infestation of roundworms, you might be able to see them expelled in their feces. They look like thin white tube-like worms several inches long. Roundworms live in the chicken's intestines and can be very harmful. These worms can cause anemia, diarrhea, weight loss, and lethargy. Flubendazole is an FDA approved treatment.

Tapeworms: These worms are easily identifiable, as their body structure is segmented. Just like a human tapeworm... YUCK! The worm eggs also look like rice in the chicken's stools. Tapeworms can get so long that they can cause a blockage in the chicken's intestines, so treatment should be given ASAP. Symptoms include weight loss, diarrhea, neurological issues, and lethargy. Chicken tapeworms cannot be passed to humans. It may surprise you though, that bugs like grasshoppers, slugs, and even earthworms can infect chickens with tapeworm... just like many of the other kinds of internal worms chickens can contract. Valbazen and Safeguard will treat this.

Gapeworms: Gapeworms are thin tiny red worms that attach themselves to a chicken's trachea. This can cause a chicken to be open mouth breathing, excessive yawning, wheezing, and shaking their head. If you think your chicken may have gapeworm, you can carefully look down their throat with a flashlight, and you might be able to see the thin red worms with your naked eye. As always, it is best to confirm with a stool sample check. Flubendazole, ivermectin paste, and valbazen are proper treatments to eradicate these worms.

Cecal worms: These are small worms that live in the ceca pouches of the chicken's intestinal tract. They don't cause as much damage to the chicken's body as other worms, but they can be a host for the protozoa that cause blackhead disease in turkeys. (This is often why some people do not recommend keeping turkeys with chickens, but if you are diligent about checking for worms, it can be avoided and they *can* coexist.) An overload of these worms can make a chicken appear sick though, and fenbendazole or Valbazen would be an effective treatment.

Capillary worms: Capillary worms are often also called threadworms because they are very thin and thread-like. They can infect several areas of the chicken's body including the crop, throat, and/or intestines. The worms burrow into the tissues and can cause lethargy, bloody stools, and diarrhea. Fenbendazole is an FDA-approved treatment and Valbazen will also work, while there are mixed reviews on whether or not ivermectin paste will be effective.

Enjoy Your Flock!

Once you get into a routine with your flock, you will find that chicken keeping doesn't have to be difficult. I find spending time with my chickens is a huge stress reliever. Even though I have twenty-five of them, they each seem to have a different personality and uniqueness. In the beginning, when I would find a sick chicken, I would be full of worry and sometimes panic. I learned early on that if I did enough research, and formed a plan, I could become more efficient and fast at fixing any problems. Never get too stressed out, and take things one step at a time.

(Two of my older chickens beside one of my
rescued turkeys)

Many of my chickens are now ten years old.
Considering that the flock went through Marek's
disease, mycoplasma, and other issues, I consider
this an accomplishment that my chickens have
reached senior age. As chickens get older, they
can get the same kind of ailments that humans can.

I have a nine-year-old Wyandotte with arthritis, for example, and although her toe joints are a bit crooked, and she's a little slower, she is still happy and doing well otherwise. Turmeric can help with pain and swelling for any chickens that may have arthritis. They can also have a bit of glucosamine too.

Some hens may develop fluid retention or water belly as they get older. As previously mentioned, this can be more common with production breeds. For this, I put just a pinch of milk thistle powder per gallon of water. I noticed that once I added this in the water a couple of times per week, the size of the water belly mass would reduce in size. Since many chicken ailments can be similar to human ailments, I now have a two-step process in my research.

Let's take gout for example… step one would be doing an online search for "what treats gout in humans". Oftentimes tart cherry powder comes up in search results. Step two is searching if chickens can have tart cherry powder. I usually follow this up by trying to find university study articles regarding chickens and the particular treatment. Part of the reason I do this process is because there are far more articles available about using all-natural remedies for humans versus articles about chickens.

I recently did a poultry presentation at my local library, and after I was done speaking, I started to worry that after I spoke so much about what can go wrong with chickens' health, I turned people off to the idea of even having chickens. A middle-aged couple had even left early, who had already been on the fence about starting a flock. I felt bad, as that was definitely not my intent. I do not want you, as the reader to feel discouraged either. Being educated and prepared will prevent many of the issues covered in this book.

I know that you can and will be successful. One of the things I enjoy most is when my chickens run up to greet me, especially the ones who enjoy being pet and held. Once you have a healthy established flock, chicken keeping is both rewarding and fun. I wish you many years of happiness watching them grow and get attached to you. Always make time to enjoy your flock!

Made in the USA
Monee, IL
25 September 2024

66602377R00069